RETURNED

A Parent's Journey in Prayer for the Prodigal

CORLISS J. MYERS

Published by So It Is Written, LLC
Rochester, MI
SoItIsWritten.net

Edited by: So It Is Written – www.SoItIsWritten.net

Formatting: Ya Ya Ya Creative – YaYaYaCreative@gmail.com

ISBN: 979-8-9912588-8-3

LCCN: 2025906783

PRINTED AND BOUND IN THE UNITED STATES OF AMERICA

Dedication

To every parent who has sat in fear and silence,
struggling for answers, you are not alone.
We are breaking the silence.
May you find hope and encouragement as you
witness God's redemptive power to heal and restore.
Yes! All of the glory belongs to God!

Foreword

$\mathcal{L}$ ife has a way of bringing us to our knees, and few journeys illustrate this truth more profoundly than that of a mother fighting for her child. In this deeply moving and transparent account, Corliss Myers shares her struggles as a mother trying to guide a wayward daughter. Through moments of heartbreak, desperate prayers, and the relentless desire to control what only God could, she learned that true surrender is the key to peace.

Corliss is not only a dear friend, but also an anointed minister, an intercessor, and a prophetic voice who has been used mightily in my own life. Her wisdom and unwavering faith have inspired many, and now, through the pages of this book, she extends that same encouragement to you.

This is more than a story. It is a testimony of God's faithfulness, His grace, and His power to transform both a mother and her child. Whether you are a parent standing in the gap for a loved one, or someone searching for hope in the midst of uncertainty, you will find strength in these words.

Prepare to be blessed, challenged and changed.

Pastor Kent Jackson
Family Life Church

Praise for Returned

*I*have known Corliss Myers for several years now and can tell you that she is a devoted and anointed Christian. She's the real deal when it comes to intercessors. She is a woman who dares to believe the promises of God's Word.

As a parent of a child who was wayward, I have personally witnessed Corliss hold on to the porch and the altar, and cry out in intercession, for her seed and the seed of many other parents. Her prayers, travail, strategy and tears have watered many seeds, including her own. Her testimony of what God has done is absolutely mind blowing.

Corliss understood that there is an assignment to see children surrender their lives fully to God. It is about legacy. It is about the generations. Who will war for our children? Who will ensure that they walk in their God-given identity and purpose?

For parents who think it's over, and those of you who feel like throwing in the towel, don't! This book will cause your baby to leap once more. A righteous indignation will rise up within you to say, "Not on my watch will my child die prematurely! Not on my watch will the enemy distort who my child is called to be!"

There will be a stirring within you to intercede like never before as you secure victory for your own bloodline and the generations to come.

The oil on this book is unmatched. Get ready to dive into these pages. Be prepared to be transformed as a parent, guardian or caregiver.

Prophetess Joanne Goddard
Embassy City Church

Acknowledgments

We are in unprecedented times. Never would I have imagined the fight for our children would be so fierce. We are battling wickedness in high places in media, entertainment, education, healthcare and other industries—all of this while maintaining the responsibility of a parent or caregiver. Many of us are still struggling with our own generational bondage and personal failures. I'm flesh and blood, just like you. I found myself fighting for my life to be the mother my daughter needed me to be. I had to overcome enormous regret and depression, and I had to learn to let God make me. I had no real answers, and I didn't even know how to find them. All I knew was that I couldn't sit on the sidelines and do nothing. This is my story of how the Father walked me through and transformed my very shattered life while transforming my daughter's, too. My prayer is while you journey with me, you will find hope in the word and grab hold of the promises of God while learning how to masterfully war with the Word.

Special thanks to the following people who have significantly impacted my journey. My husband, Danny Myers, keeps me afloat with his intercessory prayers and encouragement day and night. My mother, the matriarch of the family, Albernett Johnson, my sister, Jacqueline Mitchell who said, "You haven't lost her." Prophetess Joanne Goddard, thank you for laboring in prayer. To my former church, Embassy City, and every person who sent prayers up, thank you!

Table of Contents

CHAPTER 1
Den of Denial

It was a warm summer day, and it was almost time for her arrival. When I found out I was having a girl, I was so happy. I purchased the fluffiest girly dress! It was adorable. I already had two boys, so she would be my first daughter. I was a little nervous because I had only been a boy mom. Nevertheless, I was looking forward to a little lady in the house.

She was born weighing exactly five pounds, a beautiful baby girl. She captured our hearts immediately and was the apple of her daddy's eye. Nothing about that day or the moments later would lead us to believe all the pain we were about to walk through. Looking back, I marvel at God's grace that I'm still standing with a right mind. Surely, the enemy tried to destroy it along with my beautiful baby girl.

Jazlyn Dawn, who I affectionately call Sugar Lump, was bubbly, bright and super intelligent. Her brothers would say, "You know she's the smartest!" Indeed, she was very sharp. She excelled at school and sports. Whatever she got her hands on, we could barely keep up. She was on the honor roll, received numerous awards, and had a variety of diverse accolades. She ran a complete snack business in high school with at least one employee. My Mary Kay Directorship rubbed off on her.

I worked in banking and did Mary Kay as a side job. I spent many hours at work and tried to include my children with the second job, giving them small tasks and paying them for completion. I was tired most of the time, but I wanted to give them a good life. That was my earnest intention.

I raised them in the church, as I was. I made it my priority to keep them in church as I was burdened with giving them a foundation in God. Although I fell incredibly short, I still did what little I knew to do in the midst of my failures.

However, the constant stretching, working two jobs, and the enormous strain of financial responsibilities, as well as many other factors, caused my marriage to fail drastically, ending in divorce. The day I expressed my feelings to their dad that this was the end for me, I took a ride to calm down—only to return to being put out of the house. I gave my spare key to my oldest son, and he was not there. So, I couldn't get in. After that, I wasn't allowed to return until the court ordered it.

There was a horrific aftermath of ongoing court battles, character assassinations and violence. During the divorce, I was riddled with debilitating fear, depression, and crying spells. I was afraid of what this was doing to the children as we toggled back and forth from the family home. It was one week for me, then one week for their dad. I was ordered to continue paying the mortgage. I was scared and was just a shell of a mom, but I kept showing up. I did the best I could. A trusted senior relative advised me not to drag my children through testifying in court. I wanted to spare them the emotional trauma. Eventually, I agreed to allow them to stay with their dad for the school year. I would get them in the summer and every other weekend. I thought this would bring them some kind of normalcy and help balance their lives. This went on until they were eighteen.

The court-ordered arrangement created hostile exchanges when it was time to see the children. Sometimes I wondered if I was really going to get my time or not. There was no such thing as co-parenting; it was more like Russian Roulette driving up at the police station, hoping for a peaceful transaction.

After the exchange and pulling away, I could breathe a little. They were finally with me, and I could try to live a month in a weekend.

At one point, I was off work and saw a therapist. Often, I was exhausted and numb. *Is this really my life now?* I thought. There is so much more to the story, but this is not about me (that's for another book). I just wanted a backdrop of the circumstances that set up the plot and plan of the enemy. Satan is patient; he moves the pieces in place and preys on our ignorance, carnality and low-level spirituality. He strikes at our lowest point. Our unresolved issues and brokenness serve him well, pushing us to shipwreck.

On one particular occasion, Jaz and I went shopping with some friends at the mall. There was lots of frenzy and giggles. Suddenly, she pulled out boy boxer shorts. My friend looked at me startled. I was speechless. I felt embarrassed. I didn't know what to say. I just tried not to make a big deal of it at that moment. Later, I rationalized it. I thought it was just a phase. I wore men's ties when I was a teenager and wanted to be better than boys. I figured she would grow out of it. She explained that they were comfortable. Something about girls wearing boxers was a trend at the time, so I dismissed it. However, what I didn't understand is that this was a seed. A seed of identity. An outward expression of an internal comfortability and an agreement of masculinity. That day, I lost that battle to ignorance because I underestimated the enemy. What I thought was a phase was the cracking open of an evil door. On the other side was nothing I'd ever want another parent or child to experience.

Proverbs 14:12 (KJV) says, *There is a way which seemeth right unto a man; But the end thereof are the ways of death.*

Notes & Reflections

_____

_____

_____

_____

_____

_____

_____

_____

_____

_____

_____

_____

_____

_____

_____

_____

_____

_____

_____

_____

_____

_____

_____

_____

_____

_____

_____

_____

_____

_____

_____

_____

_____

CHAPTER 2
The Wrong Help

After the incident at the mall, many other incidents followed. Jaz told me that a young child asked if she was a boy. I said, "Just tell her you're a girl." She seemed reluctant. She wasn't in a hurry to correct the issue. As time progressed, she struggled to engage in feminine things like purses and lip gloss. She was totally against wearing make-up (except for high school pictures and prom). She hated dresses and heels, and she loved gym shoes. Most of her close friends were males. That's when I realized she was struggling with her identity.

What made matters worse is when I discovered one of her best friends was a lesbian. Jaz frequently spent the night hanging out with this girl and her mom. It was perfectly fine with her dad and because our relationship was like a nuclear time bomb, I knew if I challenged him on it, things would turn into a chess match, and I might lose total access to Jaz. I constantly battled the fear of losing access to her. It was immobilizing. The constant stress and anxiety of my life led me to drink often. I was definitely an alcoholic abuser.

When I was alone, I slid into depressive states. This was a recurring cycle for me. I felt helpless.

I knew I wanted to address this issue; I just didn't know how. I also didn't realize how infested the high school community was and the bombardment of television programming, especially Degrassi High. It was all so perverted, literally glorifying the lifestyle of the LGBTQ community. She received affirmation and celebrations from a perverse community almost daily. During this time, she didn't honor or respect my voice. I'm sure I wasn't the favorite of anyone on her father's side. I'd need to roll up my sleeves and contend in this unspoken battle solo and not expect much cooperation from her father.

In preparation to speak to Jaz, I reviewed some information. I tried to gain a better biblical perspective. As I sat down and talked to her, I was a terrified mess. I was battling my own emotions. I was baffled. *How in the world did this happen?* It was a complete disaster. I addressed the outward dress and mannerisms. I tried to manage the manifestation without touching the root of the issue. Of course, I was met with resistance, anger, accusations and bitterness. The enemy tossed me around like a wet blanket. She even tried to convince me that her dad loved her so much that he was willing to accept her in this false identity.

I felt hopeless, defeated and disillusioned. I used information from an internationally well-known Bible teacher and syndicated Christian radio and television pastor. *What happened? Why didn't this work?* I was perplexed. Even though he was right, I didn't sense much compassion from this pastor. He could explain the Scripture, but I never perceived love. He rightly divided the Word, but I didn't see tender mercy and lovingkindness. The result should be the truth that leads to reconciliation and restoration in *love*.

In the Word, 1 Corinthians 13:1-2 (NLT) says:

If I could speak all the languages of earth and of angels, but didn't love others, I would only be a noisy gong or a clanging cymbal. If I had the gift of prophecy, and if I understood all of God's secret plans and possessed all knowledge, and if I had such faith that I could move mountains, but didn't love others, I would be nothing.

In the Word, 2 Corinthians 5:19 (NLT) says:

For God was in Christ, reconciling the world to himself, no longer counting people's sins against them. And he gave us this wonderful message of reconciliation. I had accessed the wrong help! I knew this pastor was learned, but I ignored the fact that his message had a fly in the oil.

Ecclesiastes 10:1-3 (NLT) says, *As dead flies cause even a bottle of perfume to stink, so a little foolishness spoils great wisdom and honor. A wise person chooses the right road; a fool takes the wrong one. You can identify fools just by the way they walk down the street!* So, what was released lacked love and compassion. It didn't see her pain or her brokenness. The root was still there yet never addressed. It didn't attempt to love with real intentions of reconciliation. I had missed the mark. I felt betrayed by the very people I thought had the answers. I learned many are theologically educated and celebrated in their sphere, but the truth is they're holding a form of godliness, but they have denied the power thereof (2 Timothy 3:5).

I wasn't sure what to do next, but I was determined to continue my pursuit. I searched the internet and read other related documents. My generation really didn't openly deal with this explosion of perversion, especially on this level, nor at this rapid speed. I was truly in shark- infested unknown territory.

The subject matter was culturally hush, hush. Back then, it wasn't a general office conversation, nor a soccer mom's group chat. Not even the church Bible studies formally addressed it. You had to dig with the big shovel to track down a morsel of relatable information. It was hidden in the hunt.

Meanwhile, I was made aware of some adverse housing issues, which made it unsuitable for Jaz's basic needs. Her dad sent her to stay with her aunt. At this point, I was so hurt that he didn't give me the opportunity to care for Jaz. Her aunt was chosen over me, and I was perplexed. I had more than adequate housing and income. She was moving from a preteen to a full teenager. I felt like this was an appropriate time to make the transition. So, I went to court to inquire if I could adjust the arrangements, especially due to the circumstances. I wasn't behind in my child support payments, but I was literally in an *overpaid* status. However, the judge still ruled in her dad's favor. The court added an amendment stating that, should unsuitable housing re-occur, I would be Jaz's first option. On that day, I learned an ugly lesson about being trapped in Michigan's Friend of the Court. Even with fear of potential backlash and retaliation, I earnestly fought for her to come stay with me. In my opinion, they never supplied a reasonable explanation for their hard denial. I felt like I failed her, and I was utterly devasted!

I couldn't leave my baby girl in that state. I was desperate to see her free and I had to find some help. I had no idea how God was weaving this tapestry. He was in the background. He was there, turning things around and preparing to make a pivotal move! God was preparing for her moment of return.

TIME TO REFLECT

Notes & Reflections

_____

_____

_____

_____

_____

_____

_____

_____

_____

_____

_____

_____

_____

_____

_____

_____

_____

_____

_____

_____

_____

_____

_____

_____

_____

_____

_____

_____

_____

_____

_____

_____

_____

_____

_____

_____

_____

CHAPTER 3

Limited Resources

*I*was on a full quest for answers. I found a few resources, mostly online. One story left me more discouraged after I read it. I knew that wasn't the connection for me. Basically, the woman was okay with giving up. She had made peace with her child's situation. That's not what my Bible instructs me to do though! On the contrary, I knew I needed to stand in the gap. In a later chapter, I will testify of how the Holy Spirit began to lead, guide and teach me the ministry of prayer and intercession!

Matthew 7:7 (NLT) says, *Keep on asking, and you will receive what you ask for. Keep on seeking, and you will find. Keep on knocking, and the door will be opened to you.* James 5:16 (NLT) says, *Confess your sins to each other and pray for each other so that you may be healed. The earnest prayer of a righteous person has great power and produces wonderful results.*

Eventually, I found Janet Boyce's ministry. She was an ex-lesbian and a born-again believer. Her ministry supported those coming out of alternative lifestyles, so I reached out to her. We actually spoke on the phone, and Jaz spoke to her, as well. I was happy to finally find real help. Although it looked promising, I don't think Jaz was there yet. She was comfortable with her crew. What I eventually realized was this was a strong, aggressive spirit that had been unleashed upon this generation. It was a principality from Hell that is relentless in destroying a generation of children and even the nations of men and women.

The last thing I remember Janet saying to me wasn't exactly encouraging. It was a strong warning that I needed to move quickly. Time was of the essence. The longer I waited, the more difficult it would be. Honestly speaking, that caused much uneasiness. I saw her as one who spoke from experience. It simply rattled me.

I became more focused and determined at attending church and growing in my faith. I took advantage of overtime at my job, but I clearly heard the Lord say, "Sacrifice the money and go to church service with Jaz."

So, on Wednesday nights, we were both in service. I knew this was a necessary spiritual move. God was doing a work in Jaz's heart and His Word will never return void. I knew she needed to see her mom worship the true and living God. Janet Boyce said time was of the essence, so I used it to maximize her exposure to the Word. I wasn't going to *send* her. We walked into the house of the Lord *together*. I wanted my life to testify that I wasn't the same mom who was bound by alcohol or bitterness toward her dad. I wanted my life to testify that God can change a heart and restore a life. It took time. God wanted me to sow my time with Him and invest it into her. Our God is a God of multiplication. Even though there wasn't a lot of time left before she would go to college, God can do much with little. He surely *did*. He used it *magnanimously!*

Notes & Reflections

_____

_____

_____

_____

_____

_____

_____

_____

_____

_____

_____

_____

_____

_____

_____

_____

_____

_____

_____

_____

_____

_____

_____

_____

_____

_____

_____

_____

_____

_____

_____

_____

_____

_____

_____

_____

CHAPTER 4

Divine Connections

*T*he next person I met was Prophetess Sophia Ruffin-Wilson. My husband actually found her on Periscope. She was transparent and she vividly shared her testimony of deliverance from a lesbian lifestyle. Seeing her transformation and zeal for the Lord gave me so much hope for my daughter. She came to Atlanta to speak at a conference, and my husband and I went to meet her personally. I knew it was possible. If God did it for Prophetess Sophia, He could do it for Jazlyn.

Prophetess Sophia was kind and compassionate. She rounded up a few mothers who were all dealing with the same issue with their child, and she connected us. It was so strengthening being in a group where people didn't automatically prejudge you and make you feel less than a mom because your child was struggling with this particular deception. Everyone respected us and showed us compassion. They acknowledged that our pain was real and stood with us. It was a blessing to find a community of parents who didn't cast you away or give you the side eye in judgment.

Prophetess Sophia even reached out to Jaz (insert a real tear here … she is so thoughtful). She also counseled me in how to respond to Jaz. The Lord connected me to a true laborer, a genuine helper. This was answered prayers. Prophetess Sophia also followed up with me to encourage and assess the current gravity of the situation, which brought much hope to my heart. She was a relevant forerunner in setting a generation free. She is a prophet to the nations and the world would soon see it. God, in His lovingkindness, allowed Jaz and I to have close proximity to this gift. No one could imagine how much greater the impact Prophetess Sophia had in Jaz's life!

Jaz and I attended a conference in Chicago that Prophetess Sophia hosted. I was a little nervous asking Jaz, but she accepted. I was thrilled and excited. Even though our trip began a little rocky, it ended very well. Jaz met a wonderful Christian woman known as "Judge" who is now an ordained pastor. This was yet another godly connection. She has encouraged Jaz, and it has been a blessing to me knowing she's in Jaz's destiny camp.

During our time at the hotel, Jaz confided in me about her recent failed relationship. She was pretty broken up over it. There was no need in me offering her my opinion. It was time for me to simply show up as her mom. I held my daughter in my arms, acknowledging her pain as her mother. I wanted her to know that I loved her, even if I didn't agree with her current lifestyle choices. I wanted her to know my love doesn't waver and she's still my daughter. It was a rare moment God afforded me to love her for all the moments in the past I was robbed of. God gave me a future glimpse of the redeeming of my time, especially with her.

Joel 2:25 (NLV) says, "*I will pay you back for the years that your food was eaten by the flying locust, the jumping locust, the destroying locust, and the chewing locust, My large army which I sent among you.*"

This conference was unforgettable. Prophetess Sophia ministered and the altar was full. Jaz and I were both at the altar. For the first time, I was finally able to lay hands on my daughter and pray and decree over her life. I must have prayed until I had nothing left. I turned around and there was Prophetess Taliah Webb, who prophesied over me. We can never overlook the God-ordained people the Father sends. Prophetess Taliah is not just anybody; she is also a gifted prophetess, author and speaker.

Trust God. He will send you the right help. Jaz also told me she received a prophetic word from another prophet. Later, I made my way over to Prophetess Tiphani Montgomery to tell her my husband said, "Hello."

Jaz said, "Mom, that's who gave me the prophecy!"

But there was one prophetic sign that left me in awe of God. Jaz and I were sitting at the back of the church. Prophetess Sophia walked in and noticed Jaz. She sent her assistant back to escort Jaz to the front of the church, where Jaz sat right next to Prophetess Sophia. This let me know that Jaz was next. Jaz was coming out. She was going to walk in deliverance and freedom!

I knew I needed to hold on to that prophetic act and press in through prayer. Divine connections are real, and I praise God that He gives gifts as men!

TIME TO REFLECT

Notes & Reflections

_____

_____

_____

_____

_____

_____

_____

_____

_____

_____

_____

_____

_____

_____

_____

_____

_____

_____

_____

_____

CHAPTER 5

The Silver Sword with the Crismon Handle

*S*ome people don't believe God still speaks in dreams, but I certainly do. Job 33:14-18 (NLT) says, *For God speaks again and again, though people do not recognize it. He speaks in dreams, in visions of the night, when deep sleep falls on people as they lie in their beds. He whispers in their ears and terrifies them with warnings. He makes them turn from doing wrong; he keeps them from pride. He protects them from the grave, from crossing over the river of death.*

Again, and without a doubt, God absolutely uses our dreams to communicate with us. He showed Joseph not to put Mary away as his wife, and He later instructed him to flee to Egypt for safety in Matthew 1:18-24. Also, there was King Abimelech, who God warned in a dream to return Sarah back to her husband Abraham in Genesis 20. Finally, Joseph, son of Jacob, had a dream that revealed a glimpse of his destiny, which would ultimately place him in a position of authority and honor, resulting in the preservation of his family (Genesis 41).

So, I don't arbitrarily discount my dreams. I examine them carefully using the Word of God. Like the examples above, if they are in keeping with the Bible, I've learned to *war* with them in prayer, intercession, and decrees.

One evening, Jaz walked into my room. I firmly grabbed her arm and boldly declared, "The enemy will not have you!" I promise this declaration came with such force from the bowels of my belly! Jaz just stood frozen in place. I was sitting up, equally in shock. It was though the Holy Spirit was speaking through me to announce the divine counsel of God concerning Jaz's life. This was not an ordinary moment; this was prophetic. After I released that decree, I realized I didn't remember rehearsing the words in my mind before I said it. God allowed me to pull down from Heaven the prophetic word through the help of Holy Spirit. Through His loving desire for Jaz, she would be rescued and delivered!

Although I didn't fully grasp the entire magnitude of the moment, I knew something supernatural had occurred. God was giving me hope and His Word to remind me of His promise. The prophetic announcement was truly inspired by God and these verses came to mind:

2 Peter 3:9 (NLT): *The Lord isn't really being slow about his promise, as some people think. No, he is being patient for your sake. He does not want anyone to be destroyed, but wants everyone to repent.*

Isaiah 51:16 (NLT): *"And I have put my words in your mouth and hidden you safely in my hand. I stretched out the sky like a canopy and laid the foundations of the earth. I am the one who says to Israel, 'You are my people!'"*

Psalm 127:3 (AMP): *Behold, children are a heritage and gift from the LORD, The fruit of the womb a reward.*

Proverbs 11:21 (ESV): *Be assured, an evil person will not go unpunished, but the offspring of the righteous will be delivered.*

Jaz is the offspring of the righteous and a reward from the Lord wanted by God. Our Father is definitely in the rescuing business! Next, I want to share an incredibly significant dream that gave me language in intercession for Jaz.

I dreamed that Jaz and I were in a dojo, like in a scene from *The Karate Kid*. I instinctively knew I was there as the senior trainer, like Mr. Miyagi, to impart wisdom to Jaz, who was like Daniel from *The Karate Kid*. I stood right behind Jaz, carefully watching her handle and discover the hidden intricacies (inner workings) of the sword. It was like a substantial, weighty Samurai sword. The blade was bright silver, and it was shiny and polished. The handle was a rich crimson red. Jaz was handling the sword with amazement and wonder. She explained with revelation its many capabilities and uses. It was magnificent in her sight. I had the most comforting smile. I knew this was only the beginning. There was so much more to come.

I thought about that dream often. I felt like Joseph's father, who held the words that Joseph spoke in his thoughts, pondering their meaning. After much contemplating with an earnest desire to know the meaning of this dream, I received the interpretation. Jaz will take the sword of the Spirit, which is the Word of God, and destroy the works of Hell! That was it. This was the decree I must speak over Jaz that it may be established. She is a bold and fiery one. She will use the Word of God to destroy the works of Hell. She will use the Word of God to destroy the gross deception that plagues her generation. She will lead them to redemption. Jaz was born for such a time as this! So, moving forward, that was my confession and decree over Jaz. The Lord was teaching me how to war with the Word. A Word that came through a *dream*!

The sword is Ephesians 6:17, *Put on salvation as your helmet, and take the sword of the Spirit, which is the word of God.*

Silver represents redemption. Silver is used to buy/purchase something. Refined silver is pure.

Psalm 12:6 says, *The LORD's promises are pure, like silver refined in a furnace, purified seven times over.*

Red symbolizes blood atonement, the sacrifice of Christ's blood, which is the payment for our sins.

TIME TO REFLECT

Notes & Reflections

_____

_____

_____

_____

_____

_____

_____

_____

_____

_____

_____

_____

_____

_____

_____

_____

_____

_____

CHAPTER 6

Hannah's Prayer

I made the decrees and promises. My expectations were strong. I was looking for a breakthrough at any moment. The moment turned into days, months, then years.

Meanwhile, I still served. My church released me to do altar ministry, and I served on the intercessory prayer team. I also prayed with and counseled people inside and outside the church. One time, a mother was distraught about her child's situation. So, I offered to agree with her in prayer. The most convenient time for her work schedule was 3 a.m., but I couldn't leave her without support. So, it became a dedicated prayer time. We prayed for about a month at 3 a.m. Another mom was also dealing with her daughter's rebellion and division in the family after divorce. I took her call at 2 a.m. as we prayed against a panic attack. I stood in agreement of God's Word for her and her children.

Proverbs 13:12 says, *Hope deferred makes the heart sick, but a dream fulfilled is a tree of life.*

Here I was faithfully serving the Lord's people, and I was happy to do so. I was well acquainted with the pain of seeing your child suffering and longing for their healing and deliverance. I've experienced the drought of quality spiritual people who are willing or available to counsel and support. I refused to have my name added to that list. It was the Lord that provided me with the grace to show up for any of these assignments.

For quite a long stretch of time, I didn't see any improvement in my own situation with my daughter. In fact, although I prayed, things progressively got worse. I received concerned inquiries, messages, words, and adverse reports from family. I traveled back home and encountered with my own eyes the severe attack of the enemy on her life. There is something about a visual that will quickly sober you up to face the severity of a situation. However, it was an unexplainable grace that was afforded to me, preventing me from becoming totally and emotionally unraveled. God kept my mind. But clearly, my heart was shattered into pieces.

Transparently speaking, I cried out to God. *How long would this go on? How much more time, Lord, before her deliverance?* I saw other mothers post their daughters and heard of the wonderful times of shopping, vacationing and mommy/daughter moments. I felt so robbed and cheated of those experiences. When people asked me about her, I grasped for the positive things. However, I thought equally about her current state and felt the pain of that reality. Sometimes I retreated to the Glory Room (a designated room I had for prayer). I broke down and sobbed before the Lord. In my lamenting, I'd express, "Lord, this hurts so bad! This pain is heart-wrenching! How can I continue to serve? I reminded God about my labor and prayers. I was like a wet noodle before the Lord. I was falling apart at the seams.

Looking back, I must pause in amazement of how powerfully multifaceted God is. God answered my cry, but not as I expected. While I was asking the Father to fix my daughter, the Father was determined to fix His daughter, too … *me*! The Father turned my attention to the story surrounding Hannah's Prayer. He pointed out my shortcomings that needed to be addressed.

My desire for my daughter's freedom was fine and in godly alignment, but my motives were questionable. The Father corrected me because I was really praying a selfish prayer. He reminded me that Jaz was His daughter *first*. It wasn't all about me or her only being my daughter. Even when the Father revealed my error, I never felt like He discounted my broken heartedness or my pain. I was fully convinced He loved me and her, but I realized He wasn't going to allow me to pray amiss, motivated in selfishness and disorder. In other words, I was so distracted over my *own* pain that I hadn't truly acknowledged the fact I should've been partnering with the Holy Spirit in prayer with prophetic decrees so Jaz could take her rightful place in the Father's plan. No, He didn't want His prophet entangled in sin. He wanted His prophet functioning in her kingdom assignment.

Hannah's story held my answer in 1 Samuel 1. Only when Hannah finally stopped praying to just have a child, and she was willing to offer him up to the Lord, did things change. Then she bore the Prophet Samuel. Like Hannah, I swiftly corrected my perspective, aligning it with the Father's. I had no time for delay. With peace in my spirit, and the issues of delay resolved, I believed for speed and ultimate breakthrough. I knew there would be a great shift coming because I had garnered a *kingdom* perspective.

The Word in 1 Samuel 1:11 says, *And she vowed a vow and said, "O LORD of hosts, if you will indeed look on the affliction of your servant and remember me and not forget your servant, but will give to your servant a son, then I will give him to the LORD all the days of his life, and no razor shall touch his head."*

I had to return Jaz to God. In God's counsel, He released her on the earth on purpose for an assignment and to experience His love and fellowship. God wanted His prophet! A prophet is someone who declares God's truth to mankind. It's a person who speaks forth, a spokesperson, commonly known for their intercession and prophetic giftings such as teaching and revelation. Hosea 12:13 (NKJV) says, *By a prophet the LORD brought Israel out of Egypt, And by a prophet he was preserved.*

A Parent's Prayer of Repentance

Heavenly Father, I thank you for your lovingkindness and patience with me. I confess and repent for all the times I acted in selfish pride and mishandled the gift of my child/or children. I confess my ignorance and disobedience for not humbling myself and seeking your help in training them up in the nurture and admonition of the Lord. I recognize my error and ask for your forgiveness. Lord, please release to me the grace for wisdom and understanding so I can guide them in their now and future seasons. Like Hannah, I desire to return them to you. In Jesus' name, I pray. Amen!

TIME TO REFLECT

Notes & Reflections

_____

_____

_____

_____

_____

_____

_____

_____

_____

_____

_____

_____

_____

_____

_____

_____

CHAPTER 7
Divine Counsel

*O*nce I settled in on God's perspective and received the wisdom, I had to humbly admit I hadn't retained solid understanding as to how to execute her plan of deliverance. Time was ticking away and, still, there was no visible movement toward the Lord. I was growing weary. I really didn't know what I was doing anymore.

Sometimes I reflected on my failures, which were many. I wrestled with such guilt and shame from the past. This was a vicious cycle that would raise its ugly head to taunt me, especially in my weakest moments. I still prayed, and I also found rare testimonials by Juanita Bynum's mother and Evangelist Latrice Ryan. They shared their journeys until their daughters were delivered. I can't tell you the countless times I pushed replay to receive encouragement from their testimonies. Once again, I went back to the Glory Room, weak and heavy-laden. I poured my heart out to the Lord. I had truly come to the end.

The Lord heard my desperate plea and responded. The first thing I had to do was admit my gross deficiency in my own human ability. I had to relinquish control and place my total and complete dependence in God. I asked the Lord to instruct me how to think and what to say regarding my daughter. I had the Word and even the decree. But it's His strategy and His power that accomplishes His perfect outcome. I was simply the appointed vessel He chose to use. He would get *all the glory*!

Philippians 2:13 says, *For God is working in you, giving you the desire and the power to do what pleases him.*

I was for sure enrolled in the School of the Holy Spirit. I was terrified to make a move without confirmation from the Lord. I learned the meaning of walking circumspectly and obeying the Word, even when my logic may not understand. I learned to leave all the consequences to God!

Ephesians 5:15-17 says, *See then that you walk circumspectly, not as fools but as wise, redeeming the time, because the days are evil. Therefore do not be unwise but understand what the will of the Lord is.*

The Lord took me through deliverance through the power of His Word. He was transforming me into a usable vessel. He dealt with my failures, guilt and shame. I was my worst enemy, rehashing the old tape from an old life. The fire of the applied Word burned away the dross, as it was purged. I had to replace it with His *truth*. I could no longer condemn myself for my past dealings with my daughter. Yes, I acknowledged my mistake and took responsibility, but I could no longer live there. I could no longer make choices and accept feelings from that old place. I had to put on the mind of Christ if I was going to partner with God for her destiny.

Deliverance comes in stages. We may be good in one area, but deficient in another. In relationships, we may still be in bondage, needing the illumination of the Word. Secondly, I had to forgive myself. I had to allow myself to receive grace (God's enabling power) to walk in the authority, jurisdiction and stewardship as her mother. As my apostle would say, "Corliss, you have to give yourself permission to agree with God!" It almost sounds comical, but we probably wouldn't believe how many people talk themselves out of obeying God. We must understand that God gives us grace for this, but we are called to be ministers of reconciliation.

I began to rest in God. I was confident that as He was restoring and healing me, He was also dealing with my prodigal daughter.

As I diligently sought the Lord, and embraced every word and directive, I became a human sponge. God consistently provided strength and stamina. I was clearly not doing this on my own.

Romans 8:1 says, *So now there is no condemnation for those who belong to Christ Jesus.*

James 4:17 says, *So humble yourselves before God. Resist the devil, and he will flee from you.*

The Word in 2 Corinthians 5:18-19 says, *Now all these things are from God, who reconciled us to Himself through Christ and gave us the ministry of reconciliation, namely, that God was in Christ reconciling the world to Himself, not counting their wrongdoings against them, and He has committed to us the word of reconciliation.*

Matthew 7:7 says, *"Ask, and it will be given to you; seek, and you will find; knock, and it will be opened to you."*

As parents, God has given us stewardship (responsibility) and the entrusting of care for our children. As parents, we have spiritual legal authority (territory) to properly issue orders and decisions. We have to exercise this power in accordance with the Word of God for our children's lives. There is a spiritual scepter seen in the realm of the spirit that parents carry. It is spiritually recognizable. When the Lord gave me this revelation about the parental spiritual scepter, I was in awe. Of course, I was scratching my head trying to grasp it all.

When Adam sinned and fell in the garden (Genesis 3:9), he didn't literally fall out of the garden. He fell from his place of spiritual authority; Adam went missing in the realm of the Spirit. He lost intimacy with God. He lost his position, and he lost his authority. He lost his spiritual scepter. He gave it away to the enemy. When the Lord God called to Adam and said to him, "Where are you?" Adam was missing spiritually, not physically. This loss of status was seen in the realm of the spirit. Now let's juxtapose that to the spiritual authority of the parent. We also carry a parental scepter in the realm of the spirit. It's real and visible, like Adam had. As we align ourselves with God's governmental order, releasing the Word of God in decrees, declarations and prayers over our children, we evoke the powerful backing of Heaven. Therefore, we can expect a divine response!

Now that we understand the kind of spiritual authority we have as parents, and that the scepter is seen in the realm of the spirit, we must also remember the enemy is aware of this too. He will attempt to deceive you and discourage you from using your God-given authority over your children. Many parents of adolescent/adult children will be attacked with mountains of regret, hopelessness and guilt. They will battle feelings of shame and be stuck in cycles of wishing they'd done better or believing their child is too far gone. But I'm here to announce your scepter of legal authority is not revoked. It's still there waiting for you. If you've made past mistakes, or have a string of failures, confess your sins before the Lord and be restored in fellowship with Him. Go pick up your scepter and war in the spirit with God's Word for the deliverance of your children, regardless of their age! God wants to partner with you for the freedom and destiny of your child!

The scepter is a symbol of authority, rod or mace used by a sovereign as symbol of royal authority.

Stewardship is defined as the careful and responsible management of something entrusted to one's care.

Jurisdiction is the power of a court to judge cases and issue orders. It's the territory within which a court or government agency may properly exercise its power.

After one of my morning prayer sessions with the Lord, I was led to make this entry. I can't emphasize enough how powerful the principle of humility is, according to the Bible.

James 4:6 (NLT) says, *And he gives grace generously. As the Scriptures say, "God opposes the proud but gives grace to the humble."* He gives more *grace!* Therefore, when you decide to walk in humility, it activates the release of God's hand in your situation for the enabling power to do and accomplish His will concerning a matter.

Earlier, my husband made a wise suggestion that I purchase a doll for my daughter. Jaz shared with me that, many years ago when she was just a little girl, she brought her baby dolls to me so we could spend time, and I could play with her. Unfortunately, I was not very discerning. I completely missed this timely moment. I'm certainly not making excuses here. I simply *blew* it, and I didn't even recognize the severity of the situation.

Parents, we can't let work, appointments or busy schedules cloud these special moments to affirm and love on our children. I later found out after I mismanaged that opportunity. That day, Jaz decided to throw her dolls in the trash, and it became a timestamp of pain and hurt for her. As a mother, I had to acknowledge the hurt through my extreme ignorance. Though it wasn't intentional, I still caused far-reaching damage in the spirit, emotionally scarring my baby girl. So, I took my husband's advice. I went shopping and purchased a beautiful doll. With it, I wrote a letter to my daughter:

Dearest Jazlyn,

As I pen this letter, I'm literally holding back tears. I was so delighted at the news of your visit. I've been preparing for your arrival, thinking of all the things we would do, what I would cook and what we would talk about. I began shopping for distinct items to help make our time memorable. The doll I gave you, although it may seem odd, is especially important and sentimental to me. I remember the time you told me you came to play dolls with me as a little girl and I was much too tired and preoccupied. I didn't acknowledge you. You said you decided to throw your doll in the trash and be done with it. My dearest Jazlyn, I'm so sorry. Please forgive me. If I could rewind the time, I'd spend so many more hours playing with you and your dolls ... embracing, hugging and loving you. I know that the doll is a keepsake. But I hope that every time you look at her, it will remind you that you are my precious Jazlyn. My forever princess, I love you. You are always in my thoughts and heart.

Love, Mom

I genuinely wanted her to have something visual. Whenever she looks at that doll and reads that letter, she is reminded her mom loves her and that she is always important and worthy of my time and attention!

TIME TO REFLECT

Notes & Reflections

_____

_____

_____

_____

_____

_____

_____

_____

_____

_____

_____

_____

_____

_____

_____

_____

_____

_____

_____

_____

_____

CHAPTER 8

Where Did They Go?

*T*he ministry of burden bearers is undervalued. When you are going through the valley of the shadow of death—death of a dream, career, marriage or family--those who come alongside are precious. We tend to identify certain people such as immediate family members and close friends who take on the role of our burden bearers and support us. However, that is not always so. I learned a hard and painful lesson.

You may have assumed your family and friends would be there, but it's very possible you may find yourself standing alone. Literally, the ones you assumed would be there have completely disappeared. They have run out of steam and have depleted their faith for your situation. Jesus had a similar experience when He took the disciplines to pray, and they fell asleep. They couldn't even stay awake and pray in the Garden of Gethsemane. They couldn't share in the Lord's burden. It was solely Jesus and the Father. Job's own wife encouraged him to quit trusting God. She told him to give up and die!

I found myself having similar types of conversations with those I expected to support me. I could hear the dwindling of hope in their words. Their voices had low expectations of change based on what they saw or heard. I found myself encouraging them to continue to stay in faith.

Engaging in calls of this nature was exhausting. It was emotionally taxing to think that they were folding on me. How could they desert me when I needed them most? I was too hurt and disappointed to be angry. I had to accept reality and the truth.

The burden to stand in this capacity was given to me, not them. God allowed strength for me regarding this particular burden, and He would continue to uphold me. So, I quickly accepted that I couldn't expect others to carry what God has called me to steward. Every man is given a measure of faith according to Romans 12:3. It would be unfair for me to stretch someone beyond their own grace and capacity.

That doesn't mean it didn't hurt; it *still* hurts. The pain was very real, but I could not allow those feelings to breed bitterness, offense and resentment. I could not afford to give the enemy a foothold or an inch to legally operate. It was imperative that I remain pure and unoffended. I needed to be a usable vessel, free from contamination.

Many days later, during the course of a conversation, I received an apology from someone I had ascribed to as a burden bearer. I was surprised. The individual clearly took responsibility for the shipwreck, and I received their apology with gladness. As the Lord had already settled my heart not to hold any grudge, it was all well. But receiving the apology did put any feelings to rest that I was being overly sensitive.

Sometimes we aren't fully aware of the scope of our assignments. We are just trying to make it to the next day. For some of us, we're just trying to make it to the next hour. Heaven is fully aware of your assignment. Even when people may leave you hanging at your darkest hour, and you may be scrambling to make sense of it all, Jesus is interceding for us. The Holy Spirit is our helper. We must hang on to the promises of God that remind us that He will never leave us or forsake us. Never! (Hebrews 13:5)

Always remain unoffended.

Always guard your heart.

Always walk in forgiveness.

Always give no place to the devil.

Always be ready to walk in forbearance.

Notes & Reflections

_____

_____

_____

_____

_____

_____

_____

_____

_____

_____

_____

_____

_____

_____

_____

_____

_____

CHAPTER 9

You Better Not Change Your Decree

I was clearly in the midst of the long war! Time didn't stand still. It didn't give me a breather. It's moments like this where you learn to appreciate the wisdom of building capacity in the spirit.

Galatians 6:9 (NIV) says, *Let us not grow weary or become discouraged in doing good, for at the proper time we will reap, if we do not give in.*

The enemy is an expert in the flesh realm. He always seeks to have us operate from that lower level. Sight is the enemy of faith. If he can keep you focused on the situation or event, if he can keep you speculating in fear of the future, he is already leading you down the road of defeat. The enemy is an opportunist. He will capitalize on your unchecked emotions, feelings of anxiety, stress and worry. He also sends his agents in to drop wicked seeds of doubt, which are often disguised under the umbrella of care and concern. His objective is to lure you into agreement with the negative that you see, the negative information you heard, or the negative self-image you created. But, at all costs, forbid yourself from releasing anything that God hasn't said concerning the situation. Only say what God has said, no matter what it looks like!

We often don't understand that our prayers and decrees are like battle axes in the spirit. They untangle and cut down what the enemy has constructed.

Matthew 7:17-19 (NLT) says, *A good tree produces good fruit, and a bad tree produces bad fruit. A good tree can't produce bad fruit, and a bad tree can't produce good fruit. So every tree that does not produce good fruit is chopped down and thrown into the fire.*

Let the axe of the Lord be laid to every evil root that has germinated in the soul of my child. Yes, I uproot and demolish every evil seed and planting that seeks to kill, steal and destroy my child's prophetic destiny and assignment! In Jesus' name! Amen!

I've learned through prayer and fasting to lie at the feet of the Father. I lived in the throne room, the secret place. I've cried tears of supplication out of sheer desperation unto the Lord and the Lord faithfully answered. I knew when it was time to consecrate myself unto the Lord for the purpose of receiving grace to stand and face another day with courage to never change my decree.

I heard the Lord say, "You better not change your decree!"

With tears in my eyes, I decreed and kept decreeing what God said, and not what I saw!

The Holy Spirit taught me to legislate and enforce the Word until I saw the manifested promise. There were days I thought I would lose my mind. But God sustained me supernaturally by His spirit. This went on for some years.

Psalm 126:5-6 (NLT) says, *Those who plant in tears will harvest with shouts of joy. They weep as they go to plant their seed, but they sing as they return with the harvest.*

TIME TO REFLECT

Notes & Reflections

_____

_____

_____

_____

_____

_____

_____

_____

_____

_____

_____

_____

_____

_____

_____

_____

_____

_____

_____

_____

CHAPTER 10
Divine Strategies

After months and years of seeking the Lord, and still serving the Lord's people, I saw so much bondage. I saw so much pain—not just in my own life—but the lives of others. Serving others in prayer and grieving with them concerning their children or family members stretched my capacity in prayer. It created a well of compassion and deep urgency for answers. This couldn't just be one and done. This warfare strategy must be one of mastery. In other words, it had to work! I needed a blueprint that yielded demonstration and power!

God gave me a breakthrough strategy! He led me on a three-day fast for three consecutive months. During the fasting period, I only drank water.

Holy Spirit gave me detailed instructions, which included:

- Go on a three-day fast for three consecutive months.

- You can't operate in your emotions; God's prophet is bound (speaking of my daughter).

- Decree God's Word daily because Hell is not sleeping.

- War with the prophetic word/dream given to you by the Lord (the sword w/the crimson handle).

- Keep tunnel vision.

- Don't meditate on what you hear or see.

- Expect the Spirit of might to be released to you.

- Don't entertain lack of faith or unbelief.

- Anoint the room where she will be. Walk around and pray in that room.

I even sat in the bed she would sleep in and prayed. I saturated that room in intercession and prayers. The Lord told me there were gifts locked up in her and many others. He needed those gifts for the advancement of the kingdom. He told me to undo all that the enemy had done during the night. He also told me, "Don't just pray for your daughter; pray for my prodigals." Then, Holy Spirit gave me the following prayer points and decrees.

Notes & Reflections

_____

_____

_____

_____

_____

_____

_____

_____

_____

_____

_____

_____

_____

_____

_____

_____

_____

_____

_____

Prayer Points & Decrees

1. Deliverance

Isaiah 49.25 (NLT) says, *But the Lord says, "The captives of warriors will be released, and the plunder of tyrants will be retrieved. For I will fight those who fight you, and I will save your children.*

Decree

I come in the authority of Christ and decree _____ is delivered and set free from the hands of these tyrannical spirits of deception, rejection, rebellion, lust, and pride. I rebuke them, bind these spirits, and command these spirits to leave _____ and forbid them to operate, exist or be attached to _____ and command them to leave his/or her life in Jesus' name.

I loose the Spirit of the fear of the Lord upon _____ and the Spirit of wisdom, understanding, humility, obedience, freedom, liberty and

adoption whereby _____ cries out,
"Abba Father!"

Matthew 18:18 (AMP) says, *I assure you and most solemnly say to you, whatever you bind [forbid, declare to be improper and unlawful] on earth shall have [already] been bound in heaven, and whatever you loose [permit, declare lawful] on earth shall have [already] been loosed in heaven.*

Jeremiah 15:21 (ESV) says, *"I will deliver you from the hand of the wicked and redeem you from the grasp of the ruthless."*

Job 28:28 (KJV) says, *And unto man he said, Behold, the fear of the Lord, that is wisdom, and to depart from evil is understanding.*

Prayer

Lord, by your mercy and truth, purge _____ of all iniquity and entanglements of darkness seeking to neutralize his/her future, and make _____ a conduit for good only, in Jesus' name. I decree by the fear of the Lord and wisdom every evil sanction, ideology and stronghold is displaced and severed from his/her life and understanding prevails in Jesus' name!

2. Pray Against Ungodly Friends and Associates

Prayer

Lord, let every evil enemy agent, relationship, associate and friend and their purposes come to utter ruin. Cause their communication to fail. Frustrate them and loose strong disdain into their plans. I decree every reach and extension of evil seeking to engage _____ is violently disengaged in Jesus' name!

I decree all roots of rebellion and insubordination working in him/her are rendered impotent and ineffective. Proverbs 12:12 (KJV) says, *The wicked desireth the net of evil men:but the root of the righteous yieldeth fruit.* I decree all evil nets and instruments to ensnare his/her destiny are displaced in Jesus' name. I curse the formation of any evil alliances in his/her life in Jesus' name! I decree any recruitment campaign against him/her, and those joined to her for evil activities, are rooted out and destroyed in the name of Jesus!

Prayer

Father, I ask that you separate _____ from all proponents who partake of evil and call it good, those who practice darkness and call it light.

Psalm 1:1 (AMP) says, *Blessed [fortunate, prosperous, and favored by God] is the man who does not walk in the counsel of the wicked [following their advice and example], Nor stand in the path of sinners, Nor sit [down to rest] in the seat of scoffers (ridiculers).*

The Word in 1 Corinthians 15:33 (NKJV) says, *Do not be deceived: "Evil company corrupts good habits."*

3. Pray for Repentance and Restoration

Psalm 51:10 (NLT) says, *Create in me a clean heart, O God. Renew a loyal spirit within me.*

Psalm 32:4-5 (NLT) says, *Day and night your hand of discipline was heavy on me. My strength evaporated like water in the summer heat. Finally, I confessed all my sins to you and stopped trying to hide my guilt. I said to myself, "I will confess my rebellion to the LORD." And you forgave me! All my guilt is gone.*

Isaiah 7:15 (KJV) says, *Butter and Honey shall he eat, that he may know to refuse the evil and choose the good.*

Prayer

Father, I ask that you give _____ a desire and capacity for supernatural shifts in spiritual diet, to overcome evil appetites and demonic desires, grace to refuse evil, and the power to perform good works in Jesus' name.

I break evil links and demonic holds and influences on his/her soul that strengthen ties to evil and I decree his/her life is a conduit and vessel for good and good only, in Jesus' name.

Philippians 1:16 (NLT) says, *And I am certain that God, who began the good work within you, will continue his work until it is finally finished on the day when Christ Jesus returns.* Lord, I decree the good works that you have begun in _____ life, you will complete until the day of Jesus Christ.

Ephesians 2:10 (ESV) says, *For we are His workmanship, created in Christ Jesus for good works, which God prepared beforehand that we should walk in them.* I decree and declare, Lord, that your plans and purposes shall manifest and prevail in his/her life in Jesus' name! I decree _____ shall take the sword of the spirit (the Word of God) and destroy the works of hell.

TIME TO REFLECT

Notes & Reflections

Four Verses for the Prodigal

*J*ohn 10:16 (KJV) says, *And other sheep I have, which are not of this fold: them also I must bring, and they shall hear my voice; and there shall be one fold, and one shepherd.*

Isaiah 43:5-7 (NASB) says, *Do not fear, for I am with you; I will bring your offspring from the east, And gather you from the west. I will say to the north, 'Give them up!' And to the south, Do not hold them back.' Bring My sons from afar And My daughters from the ends of the earth, Everyone who is called by My name, And whom I have created for My glory, Whom I have formed, even whom I have made."*

Jeremiah 31:3 (NLT) says, Long ago the LORD said to Israel: *"I have loved you, my people, with an everlasting love. With unfailing love I have drawn you to myself."*

Acts 2:17 (NLT) says, *"In the last days," God says, "I will pour out my Spirit upon all people. Your sons and daughters will prophesy. Your young men will see visions, and your old men will dream dreams."*

Notes & Reflections

_____

_____

_____

_____

_____

_____

_____

_____

_____

_____

_____

_____

_____

_____

_____

_____

_____

_____

_____

_____

_____

_____

_____

_____

_____

_____

_____

_____

_____

_____

_____

_____

_____

_____

_____

A Prayer for the Prodigals

Father, I send your Word like a hammer to break up the hard hearts and I loose the fear of the Lord upon the prodigals. May your heavy hand of discipline be upon them day and night and their vitality sapped like the summer heat. Like The Prodigal Son, may they come to themselves, repent with a broken and contrite spirit, and be restored back to you. I rebuke and bind the spirit of rebellion and deception, and I command it to leave them in Jesus' name. I loose the spirit of humility and truth upon them. May your plans and purposes prevail in their life in Jesus' name.

Note: This is a format. As always, I encourage you to be led by the Holy Spirit. I strongly suggest you ask others to stand in the prayer of faith and agreement with you as you walk through this journey. Let me re-emphasize if you discover your camp getting weary, resist offense, and remember this assignment has been given to you and the Lord will supply all the grace you need to endure.

I felt so much weight on this, and I was determined to carefully follow these instructions because I knew I had heard from God. After completing the fast, I experienced such peace. I was hopeful, calm and settled in my spirit. I heard the Lord say, "You will be spending more time with your daughter." I felt like that time was going to be sooner than later. So, I texted her and said, "I will be stalking you" in a joking manner, which she received well.

The fast was over. I completed the instructions. Now all I needed to do was continue walking in intimacy with the Lord, be still and know that He is God (Psalm 46:10a). In other words, I had to partner with Him but stay out of His way with all my human wisdom! After all, He already had the master plan.

TIME TO REFLECT

Notes & Reflections

_____

_____

_____

_____

_____

_____

_____

_____

_____

_____

_____

_____

_____

_____

_____

_____

_____

CHAPTER 11
Living in the Promise

*P*salm 127:3 says, *Children are a gift from the LORD; they are a reward from him.*

Not long after my fasting and prayer directives, I asked God a question. "God, as we were spending time together, as your daughter who is tenderly approaching her Father, may I please have another chance to impart everything you have given me into my baby girl, my daughter?" I also asked on behalf of my mom, her grandmother, to be sustained here on earth so she could see the deliverance and transformation of her granddaughter. This was my heartfelt request.

Shortly after my conversation with the Father, I sent my daughter some money. Normally, I sent $25. This time, I was led to send $50. I had this unusual, yet comfortable feeling about releasing double the money, but it was definitely not without purpose. I trusted God had a plan in the works.

In the same week, I was upstairs in my home office and heard some voices downstairs. I could tell my husband was chatting at the front door. So, I proceeded to the front door only to find it was my daughter.

She said, "Mommy, I'm here to stay for about three months. I want to stay with you and grandma, alternating the time."

I was *looking* at my *promise*. I knew this was the season of her deliverance. The Father had answered my prayers. He is so faithful. On a random day, He sent my daughter right to my doorstep, exceeding my expectations. Every prayer point the Holy Spirit instructed me to pray, God answered. I mean every last one! He did exceedingly above what I could ever ask or think. When I was asking for time with her, the Father was already answering and making a way.

I dropped to my knees and wept when she briefly left that day. I couldn't stop weeping and thanking the Lord! I was wrecked all day long. I was so overwhelmed by the goodness and faithfulness of God! Only a loving God, a kind Father could be so specific and detailed to answer in such a way that you know it's Him and Him alone. No one else could orchestrate such a thing and He gets all the glory!

When she came back from visiting her grandmother, she stayed in the room. That same room the Lord had me saturate with prayer and intercession. The same room the Lord had me anoint the pillow and doors in. She had an encounter with God in that room. God spoke to her and told her what Scriptures to read. She knew it was God because she felt so small, and His presence was so massive. My daughter Jazlyn rededicated her life back to God. I'm thoroughly convinced that through prayer and intercession, an altar unto the Lord was built in that room. These are the workings in the spirit. We create godly altars by giving the sacrifice of our prayers, worship and praise unto the Lord. We kill the flesh or give up something. In exchange, we make room for more of God.

Covenants are made at an altar. I think about when Noah built the altar after the flood and sacrificed it unto the Lord. God made a covenant never to flood the earth again and He set the rainbow in the sky for a sign. We must not forget about Abraham who was about to sacrifice his only son upon the altar when God saw his devotion unto Him, and his unwavering faith unto obedience, and stopped him. He provided a ram in the bush. The altar is a place where God meets with man. May we always keep fire upon our altars, a sacrifice of worship unto the Lord. May we look forward to receiving a visitation from the Lord! The Lord's very presence is with us.

I also prayed for godly associates and laborers to connect with her. I spoke of Prophetess Sophia earlier, who sat Jaz right next to her at the conference. Jaz reached out to her and Prophetess Sophia said she was traveling, but she took the time to set an appointment the next day because she felt something special on her life. As planned, Prophetess Sophia and Jaz had their conversation and Prophetess Sophia agreed to coach/mentor Jaz thru her online platform.

Life kept getting better for Jaz. It was blessing after blessing. She got hired at a major bank and found favor with the manager. This manager took Jaz under her wing and mentored her in banking, and she has since received two promotions. The Lord blessed her with a car with no note. She started serving on the church media team in her field and the house prophetess, Joanne Goddard, has become her mentor. Finally, I am delighted to share that Jaz is enrolled in ministry school. She is set on course to be ordained as a minister of the Gospel of Jesus Christ.

Recently, Jaz and I accepted an engagement where we served jointly on Hannah's Heart, a ministry dedicated to interceding for children and bringing our prodigals home. God has truly redeemed our time. God has done exceedingly, above whatever I could ever have asked or thought! He is faithful!

This wasn't easy. It was very costly. It was a crushing and killing of my flesh as I submitted my will to his Word. There were many days and nights filled with tears. My heart was often overcome with desperation, grief, and regret. There are no shortcuts to becoming what God has called you to be and to steward. The current version of yourself won't do. You must be processed and made by God! But I can testify that the Father will strengthen you as He did me.

It was worth every intercessory prayer. It was worth enduring every moment of pain and process to obtain the righteous fruit of destiny for me and her. We are still walking on this journey, one day at a time. I purposely try not to overthink any singular moment. I process it, apply the Word, and hold fast to God's promises. I'm a daughter, a sister, an auntie, a friend, a mentor, a coach, a wife and a mother to a one-of-a-kind daughter, Jazlyn Dawn Dixon. She is a prophet of God, she's brilliant and she's beautiful. I will never take for granted this grand privilege to partner with the Father or forget how He healed me so I could be ready for this assignment. At times, I stumbled, and I wavered in my strength. I cried and rejoiced at even the smallest wins along the way. But God! He wouldn't let me give up. He kept showing up and carrying me in His loving arms right across the finish line! He promised that the seed of the righteous shall be delivered. And it was so! She returned! This is not just for me. It's for every parent. It's for all of us who are seeking restoration for our children. The Father is calling you to partner with Him so you can also see your baby rescued and returned unto Him!

TIME TO REFLECT — *Notes & Reflections*

_____

_____

_____

_____

_____

_____

_____

_____

_____

_____

_____

_____

_____

_____

_____

_____

_____

_____

Prayers & Decrees from
Prayers for Disengaging Evil Assignments (2019)

"*L*ord, by your mercy and truth, purge _____ of all iniquity and entanglements of darkness seeking to neutralize his/her future, and make _____ a conduit for good only, in Jesus' name. I decree by the fear of the Lord and wisdom that every evil sanction, ideology and stronghold is displaced and severed from his/her life and understanding prevails, in Jesus' name. I decree every reach and extension of evil seeking to engage _____ is violently disengaged in Jesus' name!

I decree all roots of rebellion and insubordination working in _____ are rendered impotent and ineffective. I decree all evil nets and instruments to ensnare his/her destiny are displaced in Jesus' name.

I curse the formation of any evil alliances in his/her life in Jesus' name!

I decree any recruitment campaign against
_____ and those joined to her for evil
activities, are rooted out and destroyed in the name of Jesus!

Father, I ask that You separate
_____ from all proponents who
partake of evil and call it good, those who practice darkness
and call it light.

Father, I ask that you give _____ a
desire and capacity for supernatural shifts in spiritual diet
to overcome evil appetites and demonic desires, and grace
to refuse evil and the power to perform good works, in
Jesus' name.

I break evil links and demonic holds and influences on
his/her soul that strengthen ties to evil, and I decree that
his/her life is a conduit and vessel for good and good only,
in Jesus' name."

Reference

Garner, S. (2019). *Prayers for Disengaging Evil Assignments.*
     SAG Ministries. www.sagministries.com.

TIME TO REFLECT — *Notes & Reflections*

About the Author

*W*hile many choose to wallow in self-pity and sorrow through life's storms, she's learned to dance in the rain. As a coach, author and mentor to many, Corliss J. Myers works diligently to remind others that they are not alone—no matter how hard the situation seems. Understanding the rollercoaster of emotions this life can bring—whether it be doubt, fear, anxiety or lack of strength—she is a walking example of what can happen when one totally puts their trust and faith in God. As someone who gives voice to those suffering in silence, and hope to the hopeless, Myers specializes in taking people from pain to purpose and promise fulfilled.

What started out as a love for writing poetry in elementary school soon blossomed into short stories in high school. Completely fascinated with words, she understands firsthand just how powerful words are and how easily they can invite others into your literary experience. I remember saying to myself I want my readers to enter into my stories with me! Intentional about sharing her candid life stories of triumph, Myers shares unapologetically and authentically so others don't have to experience the same struggles she has overcome. Committed to healing the broken, assisting parents and caregivers in rescuing their children, and building mature kingdom citizens, she proudly serves as founder and CEO of Gather at the Well Discipleship Program. In addition to hosting retreats, the program emphasizes building intimacy with Christ and discovering your true identity.

In her debut book, *Returned: A Parent's Journey in Prayer for the Prodigal*, Myers takes readers on a transparent journey of a mother's pain, denial, hopelessness, self-deliverance, and forgiveness. An up close and personal account of God's supernatural strategies and divine intervention, this book empowers readers to stand firm on God's promises and His Word when everything in front of them looks bleak. In addition to serving faithfully on the leadership team at Remnant Faith Center Church, she has also been a featured speaker at Hannah's Heart, Shatter the Ceiling Ministry, and Omega Ministries to name a few.

A native of Michigan, Myers currently resides in North Carolina with her husband, Danny. For booking or speaking engagements, email gatheratthewellinfo@gmail.com. You can also visit gatheratthewell.info.